Hid kam intae words

Hid kam intae words

Gregor Lamb

Byrgisey

By the same author:
Come thee Wiz, Kirkwall Press, 1978
Nivver Spaek, Kirkwall Press, 1980
Orkney Surnames, Paul Harris Publishers, 1981
Naggles o Piapittem, a study of the placenames
    of Sanday, Orkney (in preparation)
Orkney Wordbook, a dictionary of the dialect of
    Orkney (in preparation)

Published by Byrgisey, Birsay, Orkney

Printed by the Kirkwall Press, "The Orcadian" Office, Victoria Street,
Kirkwall, Orkney.

Acknowledgements

Carole Harvey has, with pen and ink, added a new dimension to Orkney words and I'm deeply indebted to her. Bertie Baikie, a friend from schooldays and a skilled amateur photographer has successfuly captured the feeling of the title of the book and I thank him for the special efforts he made, forsaking the combine for the camera in the middle of harvest. My deepest gratitude is expressed to the many contributors to 'Word of the Week' without whose support this project could not have been sustained. I would like to thank the following people:— Betty Ashby, Kelso; Liz Aitken, Stromness; Olwen Aitken, Kirkwall; Norman Baldwin, Leicester; Mary Bichan, Harray; Betty Black, Dounby; Laura Brough, Rendall; Arnold Carter, Shropshire; Dolly Clouston, Rousay; Bessy Coghill, Birsay; Tom Comloquoy, Birsay; Karl Cooper, Sanday; Eva Corrigall, Harray; Peggy Costie, Westray; Greta Craigie, Stromness; Jim Craigie, Rousay; Graeme Cromarty, Stenness; Isabella Cromarty, North Ronaldsay; Mrs Cumming, Kirkwall; C. R. Davidson, Westray; M. Davidson, Aberdeenshire; Alister Donaldson, Stenness; Margaret Donaldson, Stenness; Babs Elphinstone, Shetland; Isabella Eunson, Deerness; Jeanie Firth, Stromness; Davie Flett, Costa; Eric Flett, Stromness; Bill Foubister, Aberdeenshire; Molly Foubister, Kirkwall; Robert Gaudie, Birsay; Mrs Gibson, Rousay; Mrs Goar, Holm; Ida Gorn, Holm; Janet Grainger, Orphir;

John Gray, Stromness; Maureen Gray, Stromness; Ralph Groat, Kirkwall; James Groundwater, Stromness; Ronnie Harrold, Stenness; Gordon Harvey, Birsay; Mrs Harvey, Dounby; Randolph Hay, Birsay; Bill Hourie, Sandwick; Kate Humphray, Shetland; Hughie Inkster, Kirkwall; Margaret Johnston, Sandwick; Alan Kelday, Kirkwall; M. Knight, Evie; Alex Lamb, Kirkwall; David Lamb, Dounby; Elizabeth Lamb, Birsay; Ina Lamb, Dounby; Jimmy Lamb, Bury St Edmunds; Julia Leask, Aberdeen; Ina Leith, Stenness; Peter Leith, Stenness; T. Leslie, Kirkwall; T. Leslie, Westray; Alfie Linklater, Stenness; Thora Linklater, Stenness; Sylvia Livingstone, Aberdeen; May Low, Birsay; Marian Macleod, Kirkwall; B. M. McLaren, Edinburgh; A. Macdonald, St Margaret's Hope; Margaret MacKay, Ross-shire; Mary Maclennan, Inverness; Margaret Mainland, Rousay; Doris Mair, Aberdeen; Jane Manson, Kirkwall; Alistair Marwick, Birsay; Eric Meek, Stenness; Prof. Ronald Miller, Stromness; Kenny Meason, Shapinsay; Tom Miller, Stronsay; William Moodie, Edinburgh; Jean Muir, Orphir; John Muir, Evie; Moyra Munro, Wigtown; Dolly Norn, Kirkwall; Joan Penny, Perthshire; Gordon Pirie, Northern Ireland; Mrs Rendall, Westray; John Ritch, Stromness; Minnie Russell, Shapinsay; J. Rutterford, Edinburgh; J. T. Scarth, Kirkwall; Liv Schei, Norway; Ethel Sclater, Orphir; D. Scott, Sandwick, Harcus Scott, Westray; Olga Scott, Kirkwall; Olivia Scott, Glasgow; Sinclair Scott, Stenness; William Scott, St Ola; William Sichel, Sanday; Edith Sinclair, Deerness; Jim Sinclair,

Fort William; Jimmy Sinclair, Kirkwall; Betsy Skea, Kirkwall; Willie Skea, Kirkwall; Bryan Smith, Aberdeen; Irene Smith, Stronsay; Marian Spence, Evie; Victor Spence, Evie; William Stockan, South Africa; Alan Stout, Orphir; Tom Stout, Aberdeenshire; J. S. Tait, Holm; K. Tait, Stromness; Bill Taylor, Stenness; James Taylor (Leaquoy), Birsay; James Taylor (Flaws), Birsay; Robert Taylor, Birsay; George Towers, Selkirk; David Towrie, Sanday; Jim Twatt, Kirkwall; Mary S. Twohig, Merseyside; Winnie Walls, Dounby; Len Wilson, Kirkwall; M. Wilson, Sanday; Ernie Wishart, Kirkwall; James Smith Wishart, Kirkwall; Joseph Wood, Rendall; Miss Wylie, Deerness and the many contributors who wrote or telephoned anonymously.

Some of my contributors have, alas, passed away but this small book and the dictionary which will develop from it will be an everlasting testimony to those who shared with me their special interest in preserving the living language of their beloved Orkney.

Gregor Lamb,
South Waird,
Marwick,
Birsay.
6 October 1986.

Introduction

I was browsing through an Oxford bookshop one day when I came across a book entitled 'The Private Lives of English Words'. The author had selected a hundred English words and about each he had written a little story showing how the word and meaning had evolved. It would be a good idea, I thought, to attempt the same thing for Orkney words. That passing thought is now reality but more by coincidence than resolve.

For many years I had been noting down Orkney words and expressions with a view to producing a dictionary of the local dialect and it occurred to me that an appeal in the local newspaper *The Orcadian* might unearth some rare examples. But how best to go about such an appeal? I had previously written articles on Orkney dialect for *The Orcadian* and these articles had brought in a number of unsolicited word lists. Slowly the idea evolved that, if people were fed a small amount of information weekly about their dialect this might provide an incentive for them to help. Choosing one word only, the decision was made to write a little story about it along the lines of the English model I had found. I soon reaped a rich harvest, for, by the time the fiftieth seed was sown, readers had sent me no fewer than 12,000 words. It is now two years since the project started and words continue to trickle in. Many correspondents wrote to say that they eagerly looked forward to the 'Word of the

Week' and suggested that they should all be brought together in a book. It was in this way that transient thought turned to reality.

Over the course of the past two years, the entries for 'Word of the Week' have been chosen at random, the only criterion being that something was known of the origin of the word. The reader will notice from the alphabetical index that all but the letter 'z' are included and there was a great temptation to add the only 'z' word in Orkney dialect, 'zeendi', the number one in counting sheep! The letter 's' is well represented because in the Indo-European languages words with initial 's' are by far the most common. In the Orkney dictionary which is in the course of compilation, approximately 20% of the entries begin with the letter 's' and this book is a very close reflection of this figure.

The opportunity has been taken to revise some of the entries and to include as a footnote some correspondents' observations. It is my fervent hope that this small booklet will serve a twofold purpose. It will give great pleasure to older Orcadians to see in print for the first time words which they have been unable to find in any standard dictionary and to have the mysteries of their origin probed and, in most cases, explained. In keeping with the new enlightened attitude to language the young will see that Orkney dialect, far from being something wrong and something to be despised adds colour and interest to their everyday language whose origins are part of the great network of ancient Indo-European words.

Gablo

In Orkney this word is used generally to describe black beetles between half an inch and an inch long: in Scots it refers specifically to an earwig.

The word is related to the 'gable' of a house, Scots 'gavelock', a crowbar, English 'javelin' and German 'gabel' a fork. Connecting all these ideas is the idea of 'branching': a fork 'branches' at the end, a javelin and a gavelock were originally branches of a tree, the gable of a house is where the roof branches: Gaelic 'gobhlacan' is an earwig which in Orkney dialect is known as a 'forkie-tail': Scots 'gavelock' an earwig originated in Gaelic.

In Orkney the related word 'gablos' came to apply for some unknown reason to black beetles!

Gutter

In Orkney it means 'mud': in England it refers to a roadside drain or to a channel fixed below the slates for carrying away roof water.

An indignant Stenness lady told her bed and breakfast guests that there was no gutter about her house when told by them that their child's ball had 'stuck in the gutter'. The Orcadian equivalent of 'gutter' in this sense is 'spoot', hence the misunderstanding.

The word originated in Latin as 'gutta', a drop: in Old French the word 'goutiere' came to mean 'something to catch water' and this meaning came into English: in Orkney the word 'gutter' came to apply to the muddy mess associated with roadside channels.

Twenty years ago, in the Kirkwall courtroom the defendant, said that there was 'a lot of gutter around her house' and the sheriff had to ask for clarification; more than 300 years earlier the dempster or judge at a witch trial in Sanday was bamboozled by Marion Richart, who gave part of her testimony in Old Norse!

Bratto

Usually used in Orkney in the phrase a 'secky bratto' meaning an old hessian-sack used as an apron. The wearing of such aprons was very common on Orkney farms and last summer I was fortunate enough to see one in use. In some parts of Orkney the simpler form 'bratt' is used.

The 'o' at the end is common in Orkney dialect as in 'Willo' or 'Tammo' and is the equivalent of the Scots diminutive 'ie'. 'Brat' is a Celtic word meaning 'a piece of clothing' appearing in Gaelic as 'brat', a cloak, in Welsh as 'brethyn', woollen cloth and in Breton as 'broz', petticoat: English 'brat' a child is related, seemingly referring originally to the little pinafore worn by the child then to the child itself: Highland chieftains fly a 'bratach' or flag over their castle.

The original meaning seems 'a piece of cloth cut off'.

Teeick

A lapwing: also known as 'teeo', the call of the bird is 'tee-wappity-wee-ap'. In Westray the bird is called 'tee-whuppo' but usually in Orkney only the first element 'tee' is used with the diminutive 'ick' or 'o' attached to the end: the 'ick' diminutive as in 'Billick' is generally only reserved for a crescent to the south of Orkney embracing Deerness and Stromness but 'teeick' seems widespread on the Mainland.

In South Ronaldsay and South Walls the Scots form 'thievnick' is used for the Scots believe that that is the cry of the bird!

The English lapwing says 'pee-wit' and the German 'kiebitz': the German verb 'kiebitzen' is to stare inquisitively at someone's hand in a game of cards and we all know how a teeick can stare!

Leufter

'The sky is leufteran a bit noo': this form is recorded in Birsay: and at the other end of the Mainland in Deerness, folk might say there's a leufer in the sky.

A Shetlander would talk of a 'lur' in the sky. All these words are from the same root. Old Norse 'ljóri' was a hole in the roof for letting light in and smoke out. We can see relations to the Orkney forms of the word in Old Norse 'leiptra' to flash of lighting and in Welsh where 'lleufer' is light.

The word 'louvre' in English has acquired a special meaning today but its original meaning was a hole (in a roof). This word came into English from the Germanic languages through French. It was at one time spelt 'luffer' which is very close to the Deerness form of the word.

Creepie

A very common word in Orkney referring to a small stool: it was recorded in Scotland in the 15th century.

No one knows the origin of this word but we can show from related forms in the Indo-European languages what its essential meaning is: Gaelic 'crùib' is a bend, Welsh 'crwb', bent; Old Norse 'krjúpa' is to creep or crouch.

Linking these words is the idea of 'bending' or 'bent'. We are really 'bent' when we are sitting on a creepie. Just try it!

The nearest related word is Gaelic 'crùb' to squat or sit but there is no similar word in that language referring to a small stool. For this connection we have to go to Norwegian where 'krakk' is a stool related to 'kruke' to squat down and, of course, English 'crouch'.

As you can see we can't exactly prove what the word 'creepie' means but we must be very close to the original meaning.

Another older word for a special type of round creepie was a 'kringle-stuil' from Old Norse 'kringla', a circle.

It was usually made of straw and was known in Sanday as a 'fitwazzy' from Old Norse 'visk', a wisp of straw on which the 'fit' or foot was placed.

Dose

'Dose' is a perfectly good English word: we talk for example of a 'dose' of medicine.

Originally a Greek word meaning 'a giving' it was adopted by the medical profession as a 'giving of medicine' and later came to mean 'a quantity' of medicine given at once.

In Scotland it came to mean 'a large quantity' of anything and this special usage is found in Orkney. It is commonly used to describe a crowd. 'My whit a dose o folk wis there'. I have also heard farmers speak of a 'dose o kye'.

This is one example of many English words which we use in Orkney with a special meaning. There are other examples related to the idea of crowd. 'A haep (heap) o folk don't like this system'. 'The bus hid tae stop fur thir wis a pile o kye in the road'. 'Whit a pile o folk wis at the kirk tae see the bride'.

This is a good context in which to discuss the Orkney use of 'enormous'. 'There wis enormous o folk at the sale the day'.

What a strange usage! The English adjective becomes a noun and 'an enormous' becomes telescoped to 'enormous'.

Recently I heard a South Ronaldsay lady talk of a 'hushle o folk' meaning a group of people. On Hoy they talk of a 'heeshle o folk'. 'Heeshle' seems to be a form of 'hirsel' and originally meant 'flock of sheep', from Old Norse 'hirzla', a safekeeping. 'Hirsel' is also found in Scotland.

7

Ossígar

When hens are moulting, they are said to be 'in ossigar': in Shetland the form is 'nossigar' which is a running together of the 'n' of 'in' with the 'o' of 'ossigar' to give 'nossigar'. We know what this word means. It is essentially a 'cutting off' or a 'separation'. What we don't know is in what language it originated.

Old Norse 'af-skurðr' is a cutting off but does not refer specifically to moulting. Welsh 'ysgar' is to cast off but again does not relate to the loss of feathers. We have to go to France to the Breton language for the nearest relation.

There the word 'diskar' is used for moulting and 'diskar-amzer' is autumn, literally the moulting season.

The indication is that 'in ossigar' is probably one of the very few original Celtic words left in our vocabulary. The other dialect expression 'to moult' also has its origin in the Celtic languages. This is the phrase 'to be in the kobos'. A bird which is in this condition shows it 'rump' from Gaelic 'cibein', the rump of a bird.

Such phrases are, alas, about as rare as an Orkney hen today.

Meufy

This word is used in Orkney of close oppressive weather: in Scots the form 'meef' is used and also 'meeth' and 'mooth': the 'meeth' and 'mooth' forms are probably the more correct since its from these forms that we can find close relations.

The essential meaning is 'to choke or suffocate with small particles'. In the Indo-European languages we find that the related forms have an 's' prefix as in Gaelic 'smùid', smoke, early Irish 'smut', a cloud, English 'smut' a particle, English dialect 'smeeth', a haze.

The choking sense we find in Lithuanian 'smaugti' to suffocate but English 'smother' is another good example.

Have you ever heard of anyone describe drifting snow as 'smooran'? 'Beuy hid's fairly smooran the day'. In some parts of Orkney the intitial 's' is lost and people talk of 'mooran snow'. If you have such a bad cold that your lungs are almost choked you are said to be 'smoored wi the cowld'.

Bonnie Words

Many years ago the late Ernest Marwick asked himself the question, 'What is my favourite Orkney word'? He settled for 'tullymentan' a word to describe the sparkling of stars at night.

A beautiful word I would agree but my favourite from our dialect is the phrase 'bonnie words'. When I was 'peedie' I always had to say my 'bonnie words' before I went to bed. They began 'The Lord's my shepherd . . .' an appropriate prayer for somebody with my surname!

I always thought of these as 'bonnie' or beautiful words as indeed they are, and it was only later, much later, that I realised that the phrase used by my mother was a relic of our old Norn language for Old Norse 'baenar-orð' meant 'prayers'.

The old word for a priest in our language was a 'bonny-man' and the chapel was the 'bonny-hoose'. In 1595 a 'bonny-mans house' was recorded in Birsay-be-South.

Another word used for a chapel in Orkney was the phrase 'betty-hoose' or 'betya-hoose' but now only existing as a placename on the Holms of Ire in Burness, Sanday. This word is derived from Old Norse 'bidja', to pray to God. English 'bedesman' is from the same family of words.

Skrek

'Whit a skrek cam oot o har whin I kittled har!' The verb 'to skrek' is to talk in a high pitched voice and a 'skrek' is a high pitched sound from the voice. Someone who persistently talks in high pitched tones is said to have a 'skrekky voice'. 'Skrekko' was a common nickname in Orkney for such a person. 'To skrek' has the same derivation as English 'screech' and 'shriek' and appears in Scots in an astonishing variety of forms. The father of them all was probably Old Norse 'skraekja', to 'skrek'! An old Orkney expression for daybreak was 'skreigh o day', a phrase also found in Scots. This means the (first) 'skrek' of day, that is 'cock crow'. Another Orkney expression for daybreak was 'greik o day' and although 'greik' looks a little like 'skreigh', there is no connection. 'Greik' here is Old English 'grég', grey, a reference to the night sky becoming lighter in colour. 'Grey' was also used in Orkney for 'dawn' from Old Norse 'grýja', to dawn.

Líppen

'We wir lippenan yi both, come in'? So said a Stenness lady to her regular New Year visitors. To 'lippen' means to expect (something to happen) and the word is used in Scotland with the same meaning. I have also heard the word used in Orkney of a woman expecting a child. 'They tell me she's lippenan again' but I doubt whether this is an old usage. Scots also has an additional meaning 'to trust' for 'lippen' and this is in fact the original meaning of the word. It derives from Old Norse 'hlíta', to trust but the 't' of the original changed to a 'p'. This happened even in Old Norse where we find the words 'sýtinn' and 'sýpinn' used to describe a miserly person.

Skurt

Used especially in the phrase 'tae cairry (carry) in the skurt'. This means to carry something against the lower part of the body with both arms around the object. Such a burden is a 'skurtful'. Straw especially would be carried 'in the skurt' and Shapinsay folk spoke of 'skurtan the strae afore the kye'. When carrying a 'skurtful o paets'

(peats) it was common for the wife to lift up the tail of her 'bratto' and use it as a means of transport. It seems that this was the original sense of the word for we find that, in Gaelic, 'sgùrd' means not only 'lap' but also the front part of a skirt when used for carrying anything. The original Gaelic meaning was 'smock' or 'apron' but the Gaels borrowed the word from English 'skirt'. It is likely that Orcadians in turn borrowed the phrase 'skurt' as 'place for a burden' from the Gaels for the idea does not exist in English.

Anteran

A very common Orkney dialect word: it means 'occasional' and is used in this sense 'Hid's December noo and we just git a anteran egg fae the hens'. The word is used in Scots in exactly the same sense. In Middle English we find the word 'aunter' meaning 'chance' and from there we can trace the word back through Norman French ultimately to Latin 'advenire' to happen. Who would have thought that Orkney dialect had Latin words in it! Actually our dialect is generously springled with them. Even our prestigious first name 'Magnus' is a good Latin adjective! 'Anteran' is also the basis of the dialect word 'misanter'* meaning 'mischance' or misfortune.

* A piece of dialect written at the beginning of this century reads 'He's hed a sair misanter an' cinna loot for hostan'.

Gírs

A very common Orkney pronunciation of 'grass', included in our word of the week for a special reason. Most Orcadians I'm sure are of the opinion that this is an example of 'grass' pronounced wrongly. In a sense they are right but this alternative pronunciation is more than a thousand years old for in Old English we find that 'grass' was sometimes written as 'graes', sometimes as 'gaers'. Many words in our dialect show this shift in the position of the vowel. How many of you have come home late to find your dinner all 'brunt': Old Norse said 'brenna' to burn, Old English, 'baernan'. But back to 'girs' where we find it in the combined forms 'ruithy-girs', corn spurrey, 'sinny-girs' or 'russy-girs', couch grass and 'klepsy-girs', butterwort which isn't a grass. These are only a few of the combined forms. Do you know the phrase 'no worth a hen's girseen'? That is the amount of grass a hen needs, hence 'worthless'. If you are hard working someone might say of you 'Feth the girs'll no grow under his feet', one of the very rare complimentary expressions which exist in our dialect!

Aika's Fire

Don't test grandad on this phrase for it doesn't exist but read on. I arrived home one day to find a telephone message which read 'Man in Sanday wants to know if you have the word 'Aika's Fire'. This really puzzled me by its written form. Could it be a version of St Elmo's Fire, the name given in English to the phosphorescence which can be seen on objects or even people when the air has a high electrical charge? In Orkney this was known as 'miracles' or 'mildroo'. Fortunately I had the gentleman's telephone number. The word and meaning soon became clear when he said 'a net coorten yi ken, whin the buddom goes aal mouldy in the winter-time, yi wid say hid's all gin aikaspire'. Full marks to 'the wife' for capturing the word even if her spelling was a little bit awry. Another Orkney form of this word is 'aikelspeckled'. For the solution we go to Scots where 'acherspire' is to germinate, of grain: 'acherspire' really menas 'ear (of corn) sprout'. The sense of growing mouldy does not seem to be recorded in Scotland. What a lot of words we have for 'mould' in our dialect vocabulary and with a climate like ours that isn't surprising. Here's anoher 'mouldy' word — 'nilded'.* Can you think of any more?

* see page 66

16

Plícko

During the last war, an army officer went into Wishart's shop in Stromness and in a typically southern English accent enquired, 'Could I possibly have two torch batteries'? 'Surely', said the wife, 'whit size is thee plicko'? A lady wrote me from Aberdeen to ask how it is that Orcadians have a dialect word for something so modern — and what does it mean anyway? We have to go to Shetland to find an answer to this. There, a torch is called a 'flicko' and it is from this form that we get the essential meaning of the word. 'Plick' is a form of 'flick' which is a form of 'flicker': the essential meaning is 'quick move-

ments', especially of light. So we have the related Old English 'blican' to shine and Norwegian 'blinke' to flash, hence Norwegian 'blinkfyr', a torch. This seems to be the closest form to the Orcadian word. 'Plicko' must have been used originally for a lantern but I cannot find any evidence of it.*

* a correspondent suggests that the switch of the early battery torches had no contrivance for holding the light on hence English 'flashlight' and Orkney 'plicko'.

Fegs

'Fegs' is an interjection used in this sense: 'Weel, fegs ah'll hae tae go'. An Orcadian might just as frequently say 'Weel faith, ah'll hae tae go'. 'Fegs' is in fact 'faith' in disguise. The word is also used in Scotland. How can the word 'faith' take such different forms? Part of the answer we find in Shakespeare where he uses the word 'fay' for 'faith'. This form of 'faith' comes from Old French 'fei'. The word 'fay' picked up the English diminutive 'kin' or its rarer form 'kins' to give a form 'faykins' and it is from this that our Orkney 'fegs' is derived. But that's not the only form that 'faith' takes in Orkney. Sometimes the 'f' takes the form of an 'h' so we might hear, 'Weel haith ah'll hae tae go'. Scots also use this form: they even say 'hegs' but I have never heard this said in Orkney. It's hardly believable that all these forms started off as Latin 'fidere', to trust.

Cod

I had an interesting letter from a lady in Shetland who worked for many years in Westray. She kindly sent me a list of Orkney words she had learnt there and told me this amusing story. One of the farm servants had a very bad headache. Much to the amusement of my correspondent she said, 'My whit a sore head I hiv: aal I want tae deu is tae pit me head on a cod'. 'Cod' in Orkney dialect is pillow and comes from the Old Norse word 'koddi', a pillow. English used to have a word 'cod' meaning 'bag' and this is from the same root. From Stenness I have heard the verb 'tae cod ap', to wedge up in the sense of inserting a 'pillow'. Have you heard anyone say, 'Ah'm no coddan yi,' meaning 'I'm not telling lies'. This is not strictly a dialect word: it's considered English slang and comes from the word 'cod' meaning fool and probably had the original meaning 'empty bag'.

19

Soolka

'Feth lass wir oot o' wir soolka here'. So said a Stromness man to his wife when he felt very uncomfortable at a party. This word 'soolka' and its meaning, the gentleman went on, were given by his grandfather to Jakob Jakobsen, the Faroese scholar when he was collecting Orkney words at the beginning of this century. I liked hearing this little story, especially to learn that the conversation with Jakobsen went on in the little house where my own granny was born. Hugh Marwick recorded the word as 'suilkie' and explained it as one's neighbourhood or surroundings. He was unable to explain the origin of the word however and it meant nothing to me until I saw it in a wonderful word list given me by a Kirkwall gentleman. Here it takes the form 'soulka' and is explained as 'the circle of the horizon as far as can be seen or, simply circle.' With this knowledge we can say something about the close relations of this word. Gaelic 'seal' is a spot, Welsh 'chwŷl', a turning. It is just possible that here we have an ancient native Celtic word which has become fossilized in our dialect.

Twart-back

Also heard as 'twat-back', the name given to the cross-beam in the roof structure of a house.[†] The first element is most probably a form of English 'thwart', meaning 'across' and the second is Old Norse 'bjálki', a beam. Norwegian 'tverrbjelke' is also a cross beam. 'Back' is also used in the phrase 'couple-backs', the main roof timbers. 'Twartie', when applied to a child means that it is inclined to get 'cross' or ill-natured. I have also heard the form 'ill-twartened'. A special kind of 'twart-back' was known as a 'hallan'. I doot thir's no many hallans aboot noo. This word will receive special treatment later.[*]

* see page 30

† see page 86 for another reference to 'twart-back'

Vílðroo

Speaking of a farm which went bankrupt many years ago a local man said, 'Best kens whit happened, hid just gid a vildroo apin him'. In Sanday a related word 'vilyero' was recorded by Marwick with the meaning 'scattered'. From Shetland comes the word 'villareu' meaning 'foolish talk'.

In Orkney we can also say of things going wrong that they go 'a geldroo'. The 'a' of 'a geldroo' and 'a vildroo' mean 'in' as in English 'asunder' but the interpretation of the other words is not so easy. Here is an attempt. The linking words may be Shetland 'galder' or golder noisy foolish talk and Orkney and Shetland 'golder' gust of wind. The root seems to have been a lost word 'gvelder', to blow of the wind as in Orkney and Shetland 'galdry' a big draughty house and Shetland 'vill' a squall of wind. If our assumption is correct, then noisy foolish talk has a parallel in English 'wind'; 'vilyero' is scattered (by the wind); 'a vildroo' and 'a geldroo' mean 'blown to the four winds'.*

* see page 51 for a related word

Him-Har

This was the word used in Orkney for a person or an animal of indeterminate sex, English, hermaphrodite: in case it isn't obvious the word is a corruption of English 'him-her'. 'Him-har' also had another meaning. Old Orkney doors had wooden hinges. One of the hinge pieces was called 'him', the other 'har'. This is almost certainly a playful use of English based on Old Norse 'hjara', hinge. There are a number of words in our dialect relating to sexual character-istics. In North Ronaldsay, a ram with only one descended testicle is a 'sowany',[†] a puzzling word which no one has been able to explain. A horse in this condition is called a 'rigglin'. Related forms of this word are found throughout Britain and all probably come from Old Norse 'hryggr', back, from the belief that the undescended testicle was in the back. Here are some more words related to today's subject — pill, talders, boona, dintle, whirlygigger. Can you give me any more?[*]

† see page 58

* see Frazzie, page 61

C

Rittick

I have heard this word applied only to the black-headed gull but in other parts of Orkney I believe it can apply to the tern and the kittiwake. The 'ick' at the end is a diminutive so these birds are also known by the word 'ritto'. We find the word 'rytr' used in Old Norse for a kind of gull. On the isle of Lewis the word 'riodag' was used similarly. Like many bird names the essential meaning is 'to make a noise' which is certainly true of the birds we have mentioned. Old Norse 'rauta' is to roar, Old Norse 'hrot-gás', the barnacle goose is literally a 'noisy goose'. In Orkney dialect it is known as the 'rood-goose', the 'routh-goose' or the 'horra-goose', all different forms of the same word.

Yarm

According to which part of Orkney you live in this word has different meanings. In the West Mainland of Orkney, cats 'yarm' but in North Ronaldsay a sheep 'yarms'. The Norse also spoke of 'yarming' sheep for 'sauða-jarmr' was the bleating of sheep whereas 'fugls-jarmr' was used to describe the plaintive cry of birds. In the North of England the word 'yammer' means 'to wail or whine' and this comes from the related Old Norse word 'amra' to howl piteously of cats.

We have a number of interesting words for animal and bird noises in the dialect. If you go and stay the night with freends on an Orkney farm, you might have difficulty getting to sleep, what with boglan kye, clankan hens, yarman gibbies and wheean sholts especially if your own bairns are girnan and greetan.

Unkan

'There wis this unkan man in the hoose an I speired an I better speired an Ah'm none the wiser whar he wis'. This sentence reminds me of the occasion my brother was in a house in Stenness and the host, not having much success in identifying him, in despair remarked, 'Thoo'll be like mesel, thoo'll hae a name'!

'Unkan' is merely a form of English 'unknown'. Since we use 'ken' instead of 'known', 'unknown', becomes 'unkent' but the final 't' is not sounded so we have 'unkan'. It is used as the exact equivalent of 'strange' in the sense of 'unfamiliar'. This word is also used as a noun in the plural form 'unkans'. 'His thoo any unkans the day'? This means, 'Have you any news (unfamiliar stories) today'?

Another old word for a stranger was 'fremd' or 'frend' related to Norwegian 'fremmed', stranger. In Birsay I have heard the phrase 'frem fae' as in this sentence 'Ah na, he's frem fae the sea noo I doot, he's gittan owld fur hid' in other words he doesn't go to sea any longer because of his age. This is the exact equivalent of English 'estranged'.

Clankan

In an earlier 'word of the week' I suggested a 'clankan' hen might keep you off sleep. 'Clanking' is the sound made by a hen just after it has laid an egg. The word 'clank' is supposed to represent the sound made by the hen and it is related to many words in English and related European languages.

In English we talk of the 'clank' of chains: glasses 'clink' and Scots say that as you pour water out of a bottle, it goes 'clunk', 'clunk', 'clunk'. Norwegians believe that water goes 'klunk', 'klunk', 'klunk'. They also believe that ravens 'klunk': in English it is said of cranes and wild geese that they 'clang'. Bells also 'clang'. Frequently the 'n' of the word is missing so we get Norwegian 'klokke', bell and 'klukke', to cluck of a hen, hence Norwegian 'klukkhøne', a 'cluckan hen'! And I'm sure yi' aal ken somebody that's an aafil 'claik'!

Uivigar

A Birsay lady asks me to tell her something about the word 'uivigar'.

When she was peedie, she tells me, she might have been playing outside in the wind with her brothers and sisters and when they all dashed inside (for a 'piece' likely!) their mother would say 'My bairns whit a uivigar yir in'!

She meant that their hair was all over the place and their clothes were untidy. The real meaning of 'uivigar' is sea-urchin so what a lovely figure of speech this is.

The word was also used in Orkney to mean 'to be in a poor condition' or 'not in a thriving state' of an animal for example. We know that the word must originally have had an 'l' in it and would have taken the form 'uivilgar' because it has as its origin the Old Norse word 'ígulker', sea urchin.

The 'g' in the Old Norse word is explained by the fact that in the nothern languages 'g' and 'v' were sometimes interchangeable.

Tuction

A Sanday man wrote me to say that when he was at school, the headmaster spent most of his time beating the Orkney dialect out of him and here we have a headmaster collecting dialect words and phrases. 'It doesn't make much sense', he says. Orkney dialect was discouraged when I was at school too — even by Orcadian teachers.

In my primary school we were asked to write a story about a bicycle and we were all lined up at the desk while our 'compositions' were being corrected.

Ernie Carter (now in New Zealand — hello Ernie!) was standing in front of me having his work corrected. His story began, 'My old bicycle has had some tuction . . .' 'No such word,' said the teacher stroking it out and substituting 'rough treatment.'

This is a real Orkney word based on the Scots verb 'to tuck,' meaning to beat a drum. We find in the old records of Kirkwall that the town crier preceded his proclamation by 'tuck of drum.' Orcadians changed it into a noun 'tuction' meaning "knocking something about roughly and carelessly."

Sorry to hear that my Sanday correspondent had a lot of tuction when he was at school and I hope Ernie's bairns look after their bicycles better than he did!

Hallan

Some weeks ago I said that a special type of 'twart back' was known as a 'hallan.' Traditionally there were two hallans (which had nothing to do with the structure of the building) placed about eighteen inches apart at the end of the scullery of the old Orkney house and it was on these that hens roosted.

The word 'hallans' continues to be used today for the perches in a 'hennie-hoose.' The word 'hallan' is also found in Scots where it means 'partition' or 'space above the crossbeams in a house' and is obviously closely related in meaning.

In Old Norse the word 'hjallr' is a timber frame and in Norwegian 'hjell' is a loft of loose boards in a barn. It is strange how in Orkney the word 'hallan' came to acquire the specific meaning 'hen's perch.'*

* 'hjal' in Danish is 'chicken roost'.

Spulyiereef

An old lady who, were she alive today, would be 100-years-old, said (not very kindly of a neighbour) 'Hid's weel kent sheu got her man bi spulyiereef.'

Anyone can guess from the context what she meant! This is an interesting example of two Norse words of similar meaning put together to produce a new more powerful word. We find the same thing happening in English today where 'fantastic' and 'fabulous' combine to form 'fantabulous.'

'Spulyiereef' is made up of Old Norse 'spjalla' to spoil and 'raufa' to break up or plunder. So she 'ruined' him by allowing herself to become pregnant by him. Orcadian dialect has quite a few home-grown words like this made up of combined words.

In the old days when children skipped as fast as possible, they would say 'Watch me gae hid nickytobar' where the word is a combination of Scots 'nick', to beat, Scots 'tabour', to beat.

Gamfer

When the wind rose quickly in the middle of the night recently me neebor said 'Beuy I thowt hid wis makan a gamfer for a right blow.'*

The real meaning of this word in dialect is 'ghost' as in Norwegian 'gjenferd' so how does it come to be used in Orkney applied to the weather?

The word is not recorded in Old Norse but means 'again-travelling,' that is, something risen from the dead and going about once again. From this we get another development of meaning of 'gamfer,' to sign or portent. So if, the wind 'is makan a gamfer for a right blow,' it is giving us a sign or an indication.

The word is frequently used for meteorological phenomena. A broch around the moon, that is a large circle surrounding the moon or a 'sun-gaa,' a false sun or parhelion were considered to be 'gamfers.' If coorse yi might see gamfers playan by the roadside on any dark night and that wid be a sign o strong home brew.

* 'a gamfer for snow' is more common : it referred particularly to white cloud formations which began on hilltops and slid (ghost-like?) down into the valleys : this was considered a sign of snow.

Spret

'Whit a fleg I got when this man spret oot o the ditch!' To 'spret' means 'to spring up, from the Old Norse 'spretta' which means just that.

'Spretta' has the additional meaning 'to rip open of a seam' and is also used in Orkney in this sense. 'Mercy Ah'm spret the erse o me breeks again!'

The main idea behind this word is 'bursting' whether it be bursting out, bursting up or bursting apart. Hence we have the extended meaning 'cut' as in Orkney dialect 'spretto,' a peat cut off the surface of the ground.

There is another dialect word 'spretto' which today would be called a legwarmer. It was really a footless stocking and received its name presumably because the toes appeared to burst through.

Scootie

I was amazed to find when talking to school pupils the other day that not one knew what a 'scootie' is. A 'scootie' is a starling.

The dialect speaker, if he did not use the word 'scootie' would never use 'starling.' Instead he would say 'stirling.'

The 'scootie' is aptly named for it is a messy bird and the word means 'excrement.' Scots 'scoutins' is birds' excreta and Shetlanders talk of 'maas' scoots' the mess made by seagulls.

Apart from the starling we also find the word applied to the Arctic Skua (the Scooty-allan) and the razorbill or common guillemot (the 'scoot'). Westray folk have a picturesque name for the starling. There it is called the 'lum painter'!

Those who are familiar with this bird will know that it also makes a good job of painting the entrance to its nest in a wall or rabbit burrow.

The Morn

This word is commonly used throughout Orkney for 'tomorrow.' It comes from Middle English, is a variation of 'morrow' and contains the same element as English 'morning.' Little wonder that visitors to Orkney are confused by the phrase 'the morn's morning' and are quite perplexed by 'the morn's night!'

Orkney folk never use the word 'today'—it is always 'the day.' In speaking of 'the day' instead of 'today' the Orcadian is, strictly speaking, using more correct English for 'today' is a corrupt form of 'the day!' Old folks used to speak also of 'the streen' meaning 'last night.' It, in turn, is a corruption of 'yester-evening.'

Occasionally still among old folk you will hear a possessive used with the days of the week as in this example: 'I wir ower at Breckan on Friday's night.' This is the same possessive that appears in 'the morn's morning.' English does not have the form 'tomorrow's morning.'

Whitna

Have you ever wondered why Orcadians say 'whitna' as in 'Whitna wife's that wi him in the car?' Older folks might say 'Whitnafur a wife's that?' or even, 'Whitan wife's that?'

'Whitna' and 'whitan' are short forms of 'what kind of' and are found throughout English dialects. As for the intruding 'fur' (for) in 'Whitnafur,' this is common throughout the Teutonic languages.

An Orcadian might say 'Why no?' or 'Why fur no?' both forms meaning 'Why not?' A Norwegian can use 'hva for' for 'what?' and a German might say 'Was für ein auto is daß?' 'What kind of car is that?'

'Whit' also gives us the useful phrase 'Whitlike?' meaning 'How?' and the common Orkney greeting 'Whit like the day?' which a visitor has great difficulty in understanding. It means simply 'How are you?' and not as usually understood by the visitor 'What kind of day is it going to be today?'

Teebro

This beautiful Orkney word is used to describe the heat shimmer over the hills on a warm summer's day.*

It comes from Old Norse 'tiðr' quickly combined with Old Norse 'bragda' to flicker. Sometimes this phenomenon is known as 'teed-burn' in which the second element is Old Norse 'brjándi', flickering.

Any Orcadian who has a smattering of Norwegian can now understand why the Norwegian speaks of 'brag' as the 'aurora borealis'.

Orkney folk refer to the Northern Lights as the 'Merry Dancers' and Shetlanders talk of the 'Pretty Dancers' whereas the Gaelic speaker uses the phrase 'fir-chlis', nimble men!

* old folk would say: 'When the teebro's flyan. The grund's dryan'.

Híð

This is one of the first dialect words which came to my notice as a child. 'Why dae yi say 'hid' mither, hid should be 'it', a conversation which took place when I was about seven-years-old.

It is difficult to know whether the form 'hid' came from Norse or English because it appears in the former language as 'hitt' and in the latter as 'hit.' 'Hit' died out in English in the late 1500's to be replaced by 'it'.

'Hid' is also used in Orkney in the sense 'there' as for example 'Hid's a gren more in the bottle' meaning 'There's a bit more in the bottle'. In this respect the dialect ranks with other European languages in using 'it' in this sense. 'Hid' is also the past tense of 'have' so we can produce the interesting sentence, speaking of a dog and its bone: 'Hid hid hin hid hidden in the gairdeen'.

Swee

This fine Old Norse word is still commonly used throughout Orkney.

A conversation in an Orkney house might go like this: 'Don't mak such a noise about a peedie burn on yir finger'! 'Weel hid's sweean'!

To 'swee' is to smart e.g. of a hurt finger, especially from a burn. Formerly Orcadians also talked of sweean feather remains on a plucked hen and in a dry spell a few years ago I heard a farmer say that, on the shallow soil in the field his oats were 'aal swee'd'.

The grandad of them all is Old Norse 'sviða' burning and 'sviði' the smart from a burning injury. If the injury was severe and it was bandaged up it might start to throb but a native Orcadian would not use this word, he would say 'tift' from Old Norse 'þöfta' (to 'tift').

It is stange how these little pockets of pure Norse remain with us.

Duffies

When I was a pupil at Stromness Academy the toilets were called 'duffies'. The word is also recorded (rarely) in Scotland where it takes the additional form 'yuffies'. The name is a puzzle but another Orkney word may help to provide an answer.

Before the war toilets at Kirkwall Grammar School were called 'cogs', a word also used in Westray. Today when we speak of a 'cog' we think only of a 'bride's cog' or the contents but the original meaning would have been a wooden container made of staves, hence wooden bucket. 'Cog' is related to English 'keg', both words having their origin in Old Norse 'kaggie'. The word 'kag' is still used in Birsay to describe the wooden vessel in which home brew was made.

Another name for a wooden pail in Orkney was a 'daffo' which comes from Gaelic 'dabhach', a tub and, if the analogy is correct this might explain the Academy 'duffies'.

In the old Orkney house the piss cog was kept in a corner called a 'hurry' (from Old Norse 'hyrna', a corner) and human urine was regularly used for washing wool. I remember being shocked at school to learn that Attila the Hun treated his hair with urine but a lady contributor tells me her granny used to do the same thing and I believe the practice was quite common.

Runnan Raes

Tying up a parcel the other day with a piece of string and having some difficulty I stopped and decided to myself that it would be better if I put a 'runnan raes' on it.

I stopped again. Runnan raes?

Nobody had ever given me that word I thought and checking my word list I was right. The word 'raes' had never been recorded before. What a thrill to freeze in time this evanescence which, Will o the Wisp like, had been drifting through the islands for a thousand years. 'Raes' is Old Norse 'raexn', a knot.

So many people have said to me how strange it is that these old words and phrases flash through the mind at all kinds of odd times and taunt us when we have neither pen nor paper. I'm sure I've heard their mocking laughter as, once more they spirit themselves off into the darkness.

Old John Firth who wrote 'Reminiscences of an Orkney Parish' kept a notebook beside his bed and regularly got up on cold winter's nights to note down any word which passed through his mind. John's lost sleep is our gain for we can all enjoy the marvellous old Orkney word list which he compiled and included in his volume.

Purwheer

This old word came from a gentleman in Costa. 'My whit a bonny day, I can see Westray purwheer'. From another correspondent I got the sentence 'I can see the Owld Man o' Hoy prequeer the day'. Both words are the same.

In Orkney, formerly, a 'qu' was always pronounced 'wh' so a 'queen' was a 'wheen' and even today old folk in Birsay will pronounce 'Quoy' as 'why' as in the 'Whys o' the Hill'.

To those obsessed with the Norse heritage of Orkney it will come as a disappointment to learn that 'purwheer' is a corrupt form of French 'par coeur' literally 'by heart'. The phrase was commonly used in Scotland to mean 'easily' then developed another meaning 'plainly'.

Today the Scot would say 'Nae boather ava'!

Teultyir

Of the many thousands of words which Orkney people have given me over the years this presents a puzzle.

It came from an old lady (now alas no longer with us) who lived in Sandwick. Her grand-daughter had been expecting a baby and everybody was very excited because grand-daughter was 'in teultyir' i.e. 'in labour'.

Has anyone else ever heard this phrase?

When someone was in labour old folks would generally say she's 'tin cryan' or she was 'in the neuk' i.e. in the neuk bed but even these expressions are very old.

Old Norse 'tjald', really a tent, was also used for a bed canopy so 'teultyir', like nook might be an old word for 'bed' but the derivation of the word is anyone's guess!*

---

* see page 77 for a possible solution.

Horse

This English word 'horse' is of interest to the student of dialect because it does not change in the plural. 'Wan horse, two horse'.

These are a number of words in the dialect which do not change in the plural. 'Wan baest (beast), two baest'. 'Wan loaf, two loaf'. 'Wan load o' paets (peats), two load o' paets'. To be contrary we say 'Wan troot (trout), two troots'. Have you ever thought how we say 'Wan wife' but 'two weeman'!

There are a number of instances where we also use the plural form even though we are talking only of one instance, e.g. 'Ah'm hin me teeth pulled the day'. 'Oh? Hoo many?' 'Just wan'. 'Teeth' is used for 'tooth' in Orkney.

Then we have a problem with our feet too! My brother-in-law 'sprained his feet' and my wife (who is not too familiar with the Orkney dialect) refused to believe that anyone could sprain both feet at once. 'Feet' in Orkney means 'foot' or 'feet'.

English itself is not consistent in this respect for a man can be 'six foot tall'!

Hen Pen Dirlo

Sit up and take note Hughie, here it is!

A hen pen dirlo was a popular Orkney toy. Take a potato, stick big feathers (hen pens) in it, throw it up in the air and watch it dirl (turn round and round in the wind).

Another name for this toy was a 'tattie craa' (tattie crow) and a variation of this toy, simply a bunch of 'pens' tied together was called a 'pogo'.

Of the two dialect words here, 'dirlo' is related to Old Norse 'þyrla' to whirl and 'pogo' seems to have as its nearest relation, Norwegian 'piget', covered with quills.

I was confused by 'hen pen dirlo' when it was first given to me to 'translate' because 'hen pen', apart from meaning 'hen feather, could also mean 'hen enclosure' or 'hen dung'. It is easy to understand 'hen pen' as 'hen enclosure' but how does it come to mean hen dung?

The answer seems to be that what was originally 'hen enclosure' came to mean 'dung in the hen enclosure' just as at a wedding today someone might say 'Feth that's a grand cog' where they are speaking of the contents rather than the cog itself.

Lens Metters

This phrase is commonly used in Orkney and has changed so much from its original form that a skilled linguist would have great difficulty in interpreting it.

The phrase might be used in this situation. A child has been asked not to do something, disregards the advice and hurts himself. When he tells his mother what has happened she says 'Lens metters!' in other words 'It serves you right'!

'Lens metters' was originally 'Ill-ends metters' where 'metters' is English 'matters' or 'business'. 'Ill-end' is an old curse used in this way, 'Ill-end tae thee'!

Later 'ill-end' came to mean 'devil' so what mother said was 'Devil's business'!

Have you ever heard anyone say 'Lendy bit o' me's gan'!? This is the exact equivalent of English 'Devil a bit of me's going'!

An Orcadian might also say 'Feenty bit' where the first element is 'fiend' or devil.

Neester

Do you like eating Orkney cheese? By this I mean Orkney farm cheese. If it is very fresh it squeaks as you eat it. As children we called it 'squeaky cheese'.

A contributor from Holm tells me that there is a good Orkney word to describe such a squeak for as she says, a new cheese 'neesters'. And when I'm as old as her she says 'me bones'll neester'. I can tell her me bones are neesteran already'!

An old door opened slowly will neester and a child trying to suppress laughter in classroom is also said to 'neester'.

The nearest relations are Norwegian 'gnistre' to squeak or crackle and Old Norse 'gnesta' to crack or 'gnista' to gnash the teeth. As you may have guessed English 'gnash' the teeth is from the same source.

Glessie

Several people from the North Isles have contacted me to say that I haven't been able to fool them yet with a word because they are familiar with them all.

North Isles folk have been excellent correspondents and my word list would be the poorer without their help.

Today I'm going to be cheeky and give a word which has its origin in Kirkwall and therefore may be unfamiliar to people in the North Isles.

As you walk along some streets in Kirkwall, particularly in Victoria Street you will notice that each house is separated by a very narrow passage too small for the average man to walk through. Such a passage was called a 'glessie'.

No amount of Old Norse or Norwegian dictionaries would solve the meaning of this word. Old folk will tell you that this was a grand place to throw old broken glass which in dialect is 'gless' hence the passages were called 'glessies'.*

Such a simple explanation if we are aware of the old custom! There must be thousands of words like this which fool the etymologist.

* Stromness also had its 'glessie hole'.

Blaggeran

Deerness is particularly rich in old words and from two independent sources there came the word 'blaggeran'.

I have never heard this word used in the West Mainland.* It is used to describe, for example, clothes flapping on a line on a windy day. 'The wind's gotten up and me sheets is just blaggeran'.

The word is pure Old Norse from the word 'blakra', to flap.

More than 50 years ago Hugh Marwick made a collection of more than 3,000 Norse words still in use in the dialect but, this fine expressive word 'blaggeran' eluded him. So did many others and it is remarkable that half a century later they can still be recorded.

In the late 50's I visited Hugh Marwick with a list of words I couldn't find in his dictionary. In 1964 I had been for a walk to the top of Ward Hill in Orphir and on the way home was given a lift by Hugh Marwick in his old Rover car.

We talked again about words and names. These casual encounters made a lasting impression. Alas I never saw him again.

* the word 'blatteran' used in a similar sense was later given me by a Stromness reader.

Yeuk

A Sanday lady tells me that when one of the first toothbrushes came to the island an old lady was very intrigued to see it being used and inquired, 'Is yin yeuk'?

Now that's a difficult sentence for most Orcadians to translate today I'm sure, for she spoke in three languages. Is (English) yin (Scots 'yon', that) yeuk (Old English 'giccan' to itch).

The question she asked was 'Are you doing that because your gums are itchy'? 'Tae yeuk' is to 'itch' and the English word 'itch' is related to it. Dutch 'jeuken' to itch is obviously closer.

In old Orkney houses any protruding stone at shoulder level was called a 'yeuky stone' because it was used to itch the back. If you were 'skrullyan alive wi bobos (lice)' this was really necessary.

A Stenness lady who was challenged about her daughter having lice replied: 'Hid's no a healthy bairn that doesna hiv a bobo on hid!'

Skolder

Do you know the phrase 'skolderan and laughan', that is, laughing really loudly? In my book 'Orkney Surnames' I tell the tale of Donald Hemmigarth who didn't like Sunday very much:—

> 'Skoldoroldaree,
> I care no for Sunday
> And Sunday
> Doesna care for me'.

The first word 'skoldoroldaree' is an old form of 'Ha! Ha! Ha!' and is obviously derived from 'skolder'.

The word 'skolder' in Orkney can also be:— (a) a strong breeze, (b) an oyster catcher, (c) the screaming of seagulls, (d) a bad fall, especially a noisy fall.

Behind all these words is Old Norse 'skvaldr', noisy talk or Norwegian 'skaldre', to rattle or clatter. As far as the 'strong breeze' is concerned it relates to the noise made by the wind just as English 'gale' is related to Orcadian 'golder' to laugh uproariously.

'Golder' and 'skolder' are probably different forms of the same word if we go back far enough for we can also say 'golderan and laughan'.

In Evie there was at one time a house called Goldro: Firth parish could boast of a Skoldro. Both houses were probably poorly built dwellings through which the wind howled.*

---

* see page 22 for a related word.

Míscone

Here is, an Old Norse survival which I was delighted to receive.

A 'miscone' is a cake of cow dung. In Old Norse it took the form 'myki-skán' where 'myki' is our English 'muck'. Only the 'mi' of 'myki' survives in the Orcadian form today just as it does in English 'midden' which comes from 'muck dung'.

The word 'scone' was in general use throughout the North Isles for cow pats and is now fossilised in two placenames in Sanday. 'Scone Brae' is found at Nouster in Burness and 'Sconie Brae' at Newark in Lady.

It was on small elevations there that Sanday folk built stacks of cow pats to dry, much the same as other Orcadians built peats. Sanday has no peats and dry cow dung was used instead, even into this century.

Hence the rhyme:

> Ah'm been in Rousay
> Ah'm been in Wyre
> Ah'm been in Sanday
> Whar the coo shites fire.

Skvandle

'Whar are thoo been skvandlan tae the day'? This means 'Where have you been wandering today'?

The word 'skvandle' appears to be unique to Orkney but it has many obviously close relations, e.g. German 'wandeln' to walk about, English 'squander' to roam, Orkney dialect 'squander' to stagger and 'swander' to lurch. Have you ever carried a 'windling' — an armful of hay or straw tied with its own ends? In Old Norse this word took the form 'vindli', a wisp.

Linking all these words is the idea of twisting and turning. Robert Rendall in his poem 'Cragman's Widow' used the word 'vaigan' to mean 'wandering'. This is a clipped form of Scots 'stravaig' which has its origin in Mediaeval Latin 'extravagari', to wander.

Who would have thought our dialect contained Latin words! Next week we'll look at some good examples.

Tíshalago

This word is commonly used throughout Orkney for the plant 'coltsfoot'. I have also heard the plant called 'laggy'.

The origin of this word is to be found in Latin where the plant was called 'tussilago' and it is strange how the Latin name completely eclipsed the native name of this common weed.*

Norwegians call the plant 'hestehov', horse's hoof or 'hesteblomst', 'horse flower' but there is no similar form in Orkney dialect.

'Tishalago' forms are found throughout Scotland in a variety of spellings. Shetlanders for example calling the plant 'tuslag'.

Another Latin word in our dialect is 'salvendu': it must have been extremely common at the beginning of this century for so many old people have given it to me. It was used as an adjective meaning strong, 'Mak sure that knot's salvendu noo'. It became hopelessly corrupted to forms such as 'savandal' and 'savandwal', far removed from the original Latin 'solvendo (esse)', to be solvent. This Latin word, like 'tishalago' was in common use throughout Scotland.

* 'Tussilago', the Latin form is also used throughout Sweden.

Anðoo

Harray is an inland parish and was reputedly the last stronghold of the Norn language in Orkney but it didn't surprise me to find that the word 'andoo' wasn't included in a long list from a contributor in that parish.

'Andoo' is a word used by fishermen and means to row the boat againt the wind or tide to keep it in position. An Orcadian would feel quite at home in the Faroes where the word 'andøva' is used to describe this action and in Norway where it takes the form 'andøve'. The original was Old Norse 'and-óf'.

It can be quite a struggle sometimes to keep the boat in position and the Norwegian who speaks 'Nynorsk' uses the word 'andov' to refer to any kind of struggle, difficulty or even worry!

Kirsty Kringlo

This beautiful name is used to describe the long legged spider which we find in the heather. In olden days if children found one of these they would place it on the palm of the hand and say this verse:

> 'Kirsty Kirsty Kringlick
> Gae me nave a tinglick
> What shall ye for supper hae
> Deer, sheer, bret and smeer
> Minchmeat sma or nane ava
> Kirsty Kringlick, rin awa'!

If the spider left a drop of water on the hand before it crawled away this prophesied a good supper!

'Kirsty' is the personal name. 'Kringlo' is more difficult to interpret. It must be related to Old Norse 'kringla' a circle. Does it mean circular web maker or does it come form a lost verb 'kringla' to weave, related to Norwegian 'kringle' to twist?*

The intriguing thing is that 'spider' in Old Norse was 'köngur-váfa' or texture weaver. Norwegian for spider is 'kingel' or 'kongro' (dialect). All these words are probably very closely related.

---

* It might be that 'kringlo' is a lost word for 'bunch of heather', related to obsolete Shetland dialect 'kongalu', heather bush.

Plitterytildran

This word from Sanday is used to describe the rattling of the latch of a door in the wind. Here is another example of two words of similar meaning joined together to give a more powerful word (remember 'spullyiereef'?).*

'Tildran' is from Old English 'tealtrian' to sway or totter and is probably better known to Orcadians in the form 'dildran' shaking, e.g. with the cold. 'Plitter' or as it is sometimes recorded, 'pilter' is an onomatopoeic word used to describe a persistent sound like English 'patter'.

'Plitter' is more commonly used to describe the noise of someone working in water and 'pilter' can be used for the splashing of fish in water.

Plitter is also used by extension, of any watery mess. I'm sure we've all heard it used in this sense: 'My whit a plitter's aboot that wife's door'.

---

* see page 31

Keero

What we now call the North Ronaldsay sheep was originally the native Orkney sheep. Old folks in the North Isles still refer to this animal as a 'keero' which is clearly the Gaelic word 'caora' sheep. The Scots used the word 'kairy' to describe a small breed of sheep.

Whether the word 'keero' is an original Celtic word or an import from Scotland is uncertain. I fancy it is a native word for another name for the native sheep is the 'kersey'. This is the only word I know in Orkney dialect which combines Celtic and Old Norse elements for here we have Gaelic 'caora', sheep combined with Old Norse 'sauðr', sheep.

This word 'sauðr' is also the first element of 'sowany' the word used in North Ronaldsay to describe an immature ram.

The last element of this word puzzled me until I realised it is the same word as Shetland 'hwini' an immature ram, related to Dutch 'kween', hermaphrodite.

58

Surto

A 'surto' is a boggy piece of land. I was surprised to learn that this word is still used in dialect. It is well known in place-names, e.g. we have the Bog of Surtan up in the Birsay Hills and Surtan in Evie. Nearer the original is Swartageo near Evrabist in Birsay or Swartland in Sandwick.

Old Norse 'svartr' black referred originally to the colour of the soil and then by extension came to refer to the marshy land associated with black peaty soil.

The word 'svartr' also appears in 'swartback', the old word for the black backed gull and also in 'swarfarro' the black headed gull. 'Swarfarro' is a running together of 'svartr' with 'tarrock' a word used generally for the tern or kittiwake, birds which are usually confused with the black headed gull.

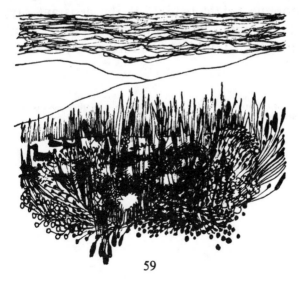

Gittan

Nothing remarkable about this week's word — it's English 'getting' but I want to make you think about the language of the Orkney grocer shop. If the shop is busy e.g. on '*Orcadian* day' an assistant will come up to you and say 'Are you gittan?'

Clearly there's something missing from the end of this sentence. I wonder what it was originally — 'served'?, 'yours'?, 'attended to'?, 'impatient'? Customers also have a habit of using 'wi yi' or 'wi thee' at the end of a sentence 'Gae me a box o matches wi thee', Gae me twa cookies wi thee'.

What the significance of this is I'm not sure for it can be left out and yet the questions make complete sense.* When he thinks he has completed his purchases the customer will say 'I think that's aboot the height o hid'. If the assistant says 'Is that aal noo', he might reply 'There's notheen ither I don't think'. Any more examples of 'shop-talk'?

---

* The missing word is 'hand' kindly supplied by a North Ronaldsay reader : the complete phrase is still used there.

Frazzie

My appeal for words relating to sexual characteristics brought this word from Westray. A 'frazzie' is a hermaphrodite. I wonder whether this word is used outside Westray?

I'm not sure about the origin of this word but it's remarkably like Scots 'faizart' 'hermaphrodite'. Sometimes in language, vowels and consonants get twisted out of position. This is called 'methathesis' and 'frazzie' seems to be an example of this. (A good example from English is 'crocodile' which in Middle English was often written 'cokadrille'.)

The meaning of Scots 'faizart' is not known and we are no further ahead in our understanding of the word, when we become aware that Scots 'peyzart' and Scots 'spuzzert' are different forms of the same word.

Our dialect is full of many puzzling words and 'frazzie' must remain one of them.

Lokkars

At one time, not all that long ago, this word was used very commonly in Orkney and I'm sure there are many people who still use it today.

Here is an example of its use: 'Lokkars is hid four o'clock already? I doot ah'll hae tae go.' It is the equivalent of English 'Goodness me!'

The word 'lokkars' is not really a word at all. It is the remains of a completely corrupted phrase. If we take 'lokkars' one stage back we get the seemingly nonsensical phrase 'lokkars daisy' also meaning 'Goodness me!' I bet many readers have heard this too!

The original form of this phrase was obsolete English 'Lack a day' or 'Alack a day,' meaning 'Woe is me!' It is also this phrase which provides us with the English adjective 'lackadaisical,' listless. In Orkney dialect, old folk used the word 'lacksadaisy' meaning 'listless.' It is remarkable that all these forms and meanings have their origin in one phrase.

Eerie Orms

I remember over twenty years ago an old lady saying she would have to get rid of a big mirror she had because she couldn't stand all the 'eerie-orms' around it.

The mirror was set in a fine mahogany frame and the 'eerie-orms' she referred to were carvings of leaves and fruit; beautiful workmanship indeed but not very fashionable at that time. Whatever happened to the mirror I'm not sure but had it stayed in the family, doubtless an itinerant Irish antique collector would have given her a good price for it today.

When the lady used the word 'eerie orm' she would have had no idea she was using a form of a Latin word. The original form was 'variorum' from Latin 'varius', varying. The Rousay lady who gave me the form 'veerie-orm' was nearer the original.* 'Eerie-orm' or 'veerie-orm' like the majority of Latin words in our dialect is well known in Scotland.

Robert Burns used the original form in his 'The Jolly Beggars' when he said 'Life is all a variorum'.

* 'fleerie-orms' is common in South Ronaldsay

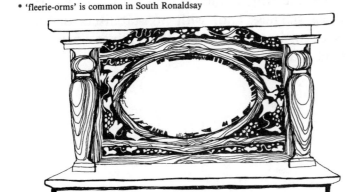

GURR

Not a very pleasant word today I'm afraid! 'Gurr' is the name applied to the slimy substance which accumulates in the corner of the eye. I think I'm right in saying that there is no word in English for this. In English we would refer to where the matter is found, 'There's a corner in your eye' or to what caused it, 'There's sleep in your eye'.

'Gurr' was also used in Orkney for fish slime and Norwegian dialect 'gor' is used in this sense too whereas Norwegian 'gørr' is half digested food. Old Norse 'gor' was used of the green frothing cud of animals and it is fairly certain that 'gor' is the old Orkney word for cud too for we find in an ancient story from North Ronaldsay that the selkie wife who had returned to the sea came back later for her cow. She went to the byre calling: 'Come oot green gorey, Wi a' thee skory'.

In Old Norse, green 'gor' referred specifically to the bile which comes up in an advanced stage of sea sickness and, with no stabilisers on their vessels, it is pretty certain the Vikings knew a lot about that!

Slygoose

This is one of many names we give in Orkney to the shelduck. Of course it isn't a goose, it's a duck but then the word 'goose' was used in a very wide sense formerly, hence we also have 'emmer-goose' or 'rain-goose' for the great northern diver.

The slygoose commonly nests in rabbit burrows in the links hence it is also called the 'links goose'. Its secretive nesting behaviour (it is said that it drags its tail to obscure its footprints!) is probably the simple explanation of the 'sly' element of its name.

The plural of 'slygoose' in dialect is 'slygeese' but 'slygeese' is also a word used for barnacles, especially on driftwood. There would seem to be no obvious connection until we realise that another dialect word for barnacles is 'klekk-geese' and 'klekk-geese' in turn also means 'barnacle-geese'!

To explain this we have to understand that, at one time, it was believed in Britain that barnacle geese were born from barnacles. Apparently in Orkney the belief was also held that it was the shelduck which started its life as a barnacle.

What a confusion of words and ideas!

Nílðeð

This adjective is used to describe foodstuffs, in particular cheese which has gone mouldy. The word is also used in Shetland where, as in Orkney, they talk of 'blue-nild' and 'green-nild', the mould which grows on cheese.

This word presents a bit of a puzzle but Jakobsen was probably right when he interpreted the word a close relation of Faroese 'naela', to sprout, of grain.

Perhaps readers will remember that, more than a year ago I discussed the word 'aikaspire'. This is another word used in Orkney for 'mould' e.g. mould on a curtain in a damp room. This word is Scots 'acherspire' which also means 'sprouting ear of corn'.

Talking of sprouting corn, 'Hid'll no be long noo afore we see the breer'. A pupil surprised me when he used this word to describe the early shoots of green corn. It comes from Middle English 'brerd' top surface.

A lady wrote me to say her father used 'breer' in this sense: 'Tak me a breer basket o neeps wi thee'. In this sense it means 'full to the brim'.

Eltit

I was speaking recently to the Quoyloo WRI and during the course of conversation the word 'eltit' came up. Several of the group knew this word to mean 'dirty'. The nearest relation is Norwegian 'elte', a mess or a quagmire. The verb to 'elt' is to toil hard at something and is also used of kneading dough. 'Elte' is the Norwegian verb to knead dough.

Another use of the verb 'elt' in Orkney is to wade heavily through something e.g. deep mud, 'He wis just eltan through the gutter'. Our dialect is rich with words for filth and dirt. 'For mercy sake beuy go an wash yir feet for they're just barkèd'. This is a derivative of English 'bark' used to tan hide.

Breek legs can be 'clarted' wi gutter (Middle English 'biclarten' to soil) 'claggered' (related to English 'claggy') or 'laggered' (possibly the same word).

The green slime round a midden is called 'iper' (Gaelic 'eabar', mud). Gaelic also has 'eabradh', a wallowing in mud and 'opar' mud on trouser legs.

Yamals

Here is a pure Old Norse word still used in Orkney. 'Willie and me are yamals: we gid tae the Oxtro School taegither and sat aside each ither in the classroom'.

Marwick records the form 'yamalt'* but I have never heard this. The original Old Norse is 'jamn-aldri' one of the same age but 'jamn-gammal' which means the same thing is a likely contender too. 'Jamn' (or more commonly 'jafn') in Old Norse meant 'even' or 'equal' and 'aldr', age: 'gamall' was the word used for 'old' so 'jamn-aldri' really means 'equal age'.

Replacing 'yamals' nowadays is the Scots phrase 'ages wi,' used in this sense 'Willie is ages wi me' or if Willie is almost the same age he is 'aboot ages wi me'.

* this form is still known.

68

Horse-Gok

This word is used in Orkney for the common snipe. A Shetland correspondent tells me that this word is also used in Shetland but for the sound made by the bird rather than for the bird itself. There the bird is called the 'snippack'.

In Old Norse the word 'hrossa-gaukr' (literally 'horse-cuckoo') was used for the snipe. Norwegians use the words 'horse-gauk' or 'rossegauk' for the common snipe and another name used for the bird in Norway is 'humre-gauk'.

The connection between the snipe and the horse is definitely the sound they make.* Old Norse 'ymr' is a humming sound and Norwegian 'humre' is to neigh, of a horse. The humming sound made by the snipe refers to the drumming sound of its tail feathers as it power-dives when in display flight.

So why is it called 'gok' or 'cuckoo'? I suspect that 'gok' is an ancient word for the bird and means 'sound maker' as in Norwegian 'gakk' to quack or Old Norse 'gagg', the cry of a fox.

* the smaller jack-snipe, rare in Orkney but common in Scandinavia makes a distinct 'clippety-clop' call in display flight.

Cubbie Roo

On the north side of the Dale of Woodwick in Evie is a boulder known as Cubbie Roo's Stone. Cubbie Roo is a legendary Orkney giant who had a habit of throwing stones around. Shetland also had its stone-throwing giants, the best known being Herman and Saxi.

It is popularly believed that 'Cubbie Roo' is a corrupt form of 'Kolbein Hrúga' the Norse chieftain who built a stronghold on Wyre. We know from his nickname that he was a big fellow for he was a 'roo' or a heap but nothing in the Sagas tells of great feats of strength. He was 'a farmer and a very able man'.

I suspect that this man's name has become confused with an Old Norse word which probably took the form 'köppu-rá', a boulder marking a boundary. Because of the durability of these great monoliths they were used as markers for boundaries long since forgotten e.g. in Birsay are the Stone of Quoyboon (Middle English 'bunne' a boundary) and Stane Randa (Old Norse 'rönd', edge). The former Stands beside the Community Centre and the latter stood near Newan Farm. Stane Randa had an older name, the Gervie Stone, probably a corrupt form of 'Gerbie' from Old Norse 'garð-bálkr', dividing wall.

Ime

All Orcadians lament the death of beautifully expressive dialect words. The passing of some words is inevitable for as society and customs change so does the vocabulary of the language. 'Ime' is an instance of this.

I know of at least one house which I can visit in Orkney and the good lady would proudly show me some 'ime' but for most of us, the advent of the electric kettle in the 1950's sounded the death knell of the word.

'Ime' is the soot on the bottom of a kettle. In Old Norse this word took the form 'ím' and meant 'dust' or 'ashes'. The actual word used by the Norse for 'ime' was 'hrím' which had no connection with 'ím'.

'Ime' is related to 'aamers' (English 'embers' or Old Norse 'eimyrja'). Because of its grey ashen colour the Norse poet spoke of a she-wolf as 'íma' whereas Orcadians used the word 'imy' to describe a grey sky. 'Hid's kinda imy the day Jessie, I doot hid's gaan tae rain'.

Toft

'It is very expensive to build a house in Bergen', advised my Norwegian guide, 'most expensive will be the tomt'. . . I'm sorry I do not know what a tomt is in English'. I cannot speak Norwegian but I do know many words which are connected with placenames so I quickly shouted 'building site' and I was right!

In Orkney placenames it takes a variety of forms such as 'toft', 'tafts', 'tufta', etc. We do not use the word any longer in dialect but it can still be found in title deeds. The original meaning of the word was an 'empty place' as in Old Norse 'tóm'.

Orcadians use the phrase 'tae teum oot' meaning to empty and we say 'Hid's teuman doon' when it's pouring with rain.

In Shapinsay I recorded 'chomheed' meaning 'a fool', literally empty head. The story was told me that, at the end of last century, two neighbours disagreed about a boundary. When one of the disputants could not make the other see his point of view, he taunted him with this insult, 'Min thoo are a chomheed and so thoo are and so wis thee faither afore thee and that son o thine is anither wan!'

Skrue

'Mercy when I opened the biscuits, they were aal in skrue'. A fine Old Norse word this, its original form was 'skróðr', a shred.

A closely related word in English, apart from 'shred' is 'shard', a broken piece of pottery.

Old folks would also say the biscuits were 'in coom' and every farmer knows that 'coom' is the name for mill dust. This word is the same as English 'culm', coal dust and probably the same as Scots 'calmstone' a (dusty?) limestone.

An old gentleman speaking to me of his early schooldays said, 'Thir wir no dinners thanadays: we just tuk a piece a' dry oatbread in wir pooch and affens whin we cam tae aet hid, hid wis all in muldroos!'

'Muldroos' is another expressive word for 'crumbs'. The original Old Norse word was 'meldr', flour. The poor chap's oatbannock had gone back to its original oatmeal!

Arroo

This word was commonly used in Orkney for a pullet. 'Arroo' was also a taunt used by German soldiers in the 1st World War when they came face to face with the Bantam Divisions and a gentleman with Orkney connections wrote to ask whether they were shouting 'pullet!' at them.

It seemed a reasonable assumption because the German language and Old Norse are related. As so often happens in language, words which have a similar sound and are used in similar circumstances trick us into thinking that they are from the same root.

The German shouted 'arroo, arroo, arroo' meaning 'cock-a-doodle-do' where 'arroo' is meant to represent the sound of a cock crowing.

The Orkney dialect word 'arroo' comes from Gaelic 'eireag' a pullet and has entered our dialect through Scots. In the early 20's, a caller at a house in Costa declared that she was collecting for 'Earl Haigs' and was surprised when the wife o the hoose said 'I think I hiv twa three' and disappeared. She returned with a half a dozen small eggs in a bowl. 'Thir must be some kinda mistake' said the collector, 'Ah'm collectan fur Earl Haigs'.

'Merciful,' said the wife, 'I thowt thoo wir wantan arroo eggs.'

TROWY

'Trowy' means sickly or in poor condition. Many years ago, Ernest Marwick, in that wonderful column 'Looking Around' said he had received a letter from a Gaelic speaker telling him that, in Gaelic, the word 'truagh' was used in the sense 'miserable' and did the Orkney word 'trowy' have a Gaelic origin?

Hitherto it had always been assumed that the adjective 'trowy' came from 'trow', the Orkney word for a goblin and really meant 'betwitched'. The original word would have been Old Norse 'troll' an ogre. A story from Birsay shows that the word comes from Norse and not Gaelic. A servant lass at Swannay had been very ill and someone had gone to visit her.

'Hoo did thoo find her?' enquired a neighbour.

'Oh I doot she's kinda trully, gullie' was the reply.

'Trully' is a very old form of 'trowy' and there is no doubt that the origin lies in 'troll'.

Brett

A school friend of mine used to boast, 'Ah'm five feet ten in me sole stockings and wi me sark sleeves bretted ap'.

That little quotation is full of interesting points about Orkney dialect but today I'm concerned only with 'brett'.

An Icelander would have little difficulty understanding an Orcadian who talked of 'brettan ap his sleeves' for in Iceland today the verb 'bretta' is used for exactly the same activity. In Old Norse it was used in the sense of 'turning up' of a tail for example. 'Tae brett ap' to some-body is used of a small person challenging someone bigger than himself.

Someone told me recently that my father (who was a small man) was wrongly accused by a workmate of carelessly trapping his finger in a cart. After being persistently accused he turned to the man saying, 'You're maybe a big man but you're also a big target'. That's a good example of 'brettan ap' and I think that here it has the Norse meaning of holding oneself erect (like a tail) rather than rolling up the sleeves and preparing for a fight!

Trimsan

'I hid tae let the boy oot', said a teacher friend, 'he wis just trimsan'. No English verb can so adequately describe the agitated state of a child needing to go to the toilet!

Specifically it means 'moving off one leg on to the other'. Farmers use the same word when they talk of a cow that is just about to calve. The cow is said to be 'trimsan' or 'in trimso' for it too moves off one leg on to the other.

A Shetlander used the word 'trimsan' in a completely different sense 'Her petticoat wis trimsan doon ahint her' i.e. hanging loosely. Both the Shetland and the Orkney words are related. The original meaning of both is 'rag' but later meanings were 'dangling like a rag' and 'shaking'.

Thinking about 'trimsan' solved another problem for me. Remember I asked for help with 'in teultyir', in labour? It is derived in exactly the same way. Norwegian 'tultra' is a rag (gives Orkney dialect 'taldery' ragged), Orkney 'teultry' is shaky and 'teultyir' probably originally referred to the agitated state of a cow about to calve, later applied to a women.

Amís

In the late 50's I was trying to find Fursebreck in Harray. Not having much success I knocked on a cottage door and to my surprise I heard a voice from inside say 'Come in'. Thinking there must be some kind of mistake I knocked again only to hear the friendly invitation repeated.

I walked inside and there was an old lady with a completely dumbfounded expression on her face. 'Mercy' she said, 'I wis expectan me neebor' then she burst into loud laughter saying 'Hid wis weel amis, hid wis weel amis'.

Now it doesn't help you very much to understand what she said when I say that 'amis' means 'alms'. In Orkney dialect we must consider the whole phrase 'weel amis' which means, roughly, 'well deserved' but only of a stupid action. This phrase is still in common use in Orkney.

Thanks to the Harray lady who gave me 'amis-bairn',* a child born after its father has died. No wonder they say Harray was the last stronghold of Norn: the Norse spoke of 'ölmusu-barn', a pauper child who had to survive by the 'alms' he received. I have not heard this word used in any other part of Orkney.

* in Orkney and Shetland an 'amis-bairn' was considered to be born with the power of bestowing good or evil. An Evie man who was an 'amis-bairn' told me that his mother was regularly given a shilling by a neighbour every time the neighbour had a child in the hope that this would bring the newborn child good luck.

Imbian

What remarkable Old Norse survivals are still to be found in Orkney. An 'imbian' is a native of a district. 'He's an imbian o Evie' (no many imbians in Evie noo I doot!)

The Old Norse form was 'inn-byggjandi' and means 'in-dwelling'. Why does an 'm' appear in the Orkney form? The answer is that, in Orkney dialect where an 'n' is followed by a 'b' the 'n' is changed to an 'm' to make pronunciation easier.

Take 'Dounby' for example: Orcadians pronounce it 'Doomby' and that part of the old Orkney house near the fire was called the 'imby', literally 'in-by'. Another word for 'dwelling' in the sense of 'living' in Old Norse was 'búandi' and the name given by Orcadians to the little people who lived in mounds was 'haug-búandi' a word which over the years became corrupted to 'hogboon' or 'hogboy'.

We know that in the 16th century Orcadians when they met addressed each other as 'búandi'. When we see two old fellows meeting today and exchanging the greeting 'Weel beuy' it's tempting to think that this is a relic of our lost language.

Week

'Week' in Orkney can mean 'seven days' just as in English : 'week' is also the pronunciation of 'wick' (of a lamp) and of the placename and surname Wick. Just to be contrary, Orcadians pronounce 'weak' as 'weck'! 'Me legs wir just weck efter a day in the paet hill'.

There is another 'week' in our dialect but it's always used in the plural 'weeks'.* 'Weeks' is the name we give to the corners of the mouth. Weren't we all told when we were peedie 'tae clean wir weeks?' The word is still in common use yet.

Our Norse ancestors spoke of 'munn-vík' where the first word 'munn' means 'mouth'. The real meaning of 'vík' is bend : it was also used for a bend in the coastline, i.e. a bay or a creek. 'Sand-vík' was the old name for the Bay of Skaill. Where we get a place like 'Anders-wick' in Stenness, the meaning would be 'a corner of land belonging to Anders'. The Vikings were the people of the creeks and bays.

* 'weekings' or 'weegings' is another form.

Wursum Mither

It's encouraging to know that many young people in Orkney take a great interest in the old words used by their parents and grandparents. That's how I started too.

I was surprised the other day nevertheless when I bumped into a young fellow who told me he had just been to hospital to have his 'wursum-mither' removed. Sounds painful. Actually it is I believe — very! 'Wursum-mither' is the core of a boil. Sometimes I've heard the word used in the corrupted form 'mother-worship'.

'Wursum' is an Old English word found in Scots too and was used for the pus in a boil (or 'booick'). 'Mither' means 'mother' here and is a strange use of the word.*

The Faroese use mother in this sense too for they speak of the core of a boil as 'vágsmóðir' a word also used in Orkney but taking the form 'vos-mither'.

The Norwegians speak of pus as 'vågmor' and the element 'mor' here also means mother. Has anyone heard the word 'meeter' used for pus? It would seem at first sight to be a form of English 'matter' but 'matter' in Orkney is pronounced 'metter'! Can anyone explain?

---

* Mother here probably means 'source' as in mother of pearl. As a student I worked on the island of Mull. I had many warts on my hands and I asked an old lady how to get rid of them. 'Kill the king', she said, 'and the rest will go'. 'King' seems to be used here in the same sense as 'mother'.

Bort

This week we have an old technical word. Few women would know this word and since the operation is rarely performed these days few young men would know the word either.

Ten years ago in Cruaday quarry in Sandwick I saw a man with great skill, bort a flag. To 'bort' is to 'split' and he was driving wedges into the rock face to try and raise a large flagstone. 'Bort' was also used in Scotland and so was the form 'brot' which is nearer the original.

This word has its origin in the Norse language as we can see in Faroese 'brot', a split, but since the Faroe Islands are volcanic there is little opportunity to 'bort a flag' there.

I was in the company of a Faroese gentleman when he saw his first stone house in Orkney. He could not believe that stone would split so naturally along bedding planes, 'These are bricks' he said affirmatively!

We also have volcanic rocks in Orkney: keep your eyes open next time you walk along Marwick beach for these dark ridges of rock. Birsay folk call them 'iron dykes'.

Sweenkle

When your belly is full of tea or other suitable refreshment it makes a noise when you move. Your belly (or should I say puggy) is said to 'sweenkle'. Shetlanders use the word too of water splashing round in a container.

That the word is Norse there is no doubt for there is an old Norwegian dialect word 'skvinkla' to splash. There are a number of dialect words for 'splash', one of the most interesting being the word 'cholter' or 'cholder'. This gives us the word 'choldro' an infertile egg. Unlike a 'burded' egg the 'choldro' splashes around when shaken.

Another Orkney dialect word for splashing around of liquid in a container is 'swilter'. Shetlanders say 'swalter', whereas Norwegians use the word 'skvaldra'. These three words are related to each other and all the words discussed today are derived from the sound made by splashing liquids.

Tud

I wonder whether this word is used outside the Marwick district of Birsay? The word exists here because it is in Marwick where tuds are experienced.

I hadn't lived in Marwick very long until someone said to me 'Yi'll be ootside the tud line there furtivver'.

A 'tud' is a very powerful whirlwind which strikes the north west corner of Marwick from time to time. Local folk will tell you that 'hid comes oot o the craig'. From Costa came the word 'tuddy' used to describe a gusting wind.

The word 'tud' is obviously related to 'thud' but it is interesting that here in Birsay it is used in the Old English sense where 'þóden' was a whirlwind.

Queebeck

In an interesting list of words which came in I found the word 'queebeck', the call of the red grouse or 'mirren' as we call it. I already had the call noted as 'tae bek' in an old poem my mother used to recite. It supposedly echoes the complete call of the mirren. It goes:

'Kitty come hame, kitty come hame, kitty come
        hame
Whit tae deu, whit tae deu, whit tae deu?
Tae bek (bake) tae bek tae bek
Whit in, whit in, whit in?
A buckyoyoyoyoyo!'

What's happened to the 'mirren' these days? It's a long time since I heard this beautiful call. Another call disappearing from moorland Orcadia (the little bit we have left) is 'poor wheeo, poor wheeo, poor wheeo', the call of the golden plover.

An old man and his son were workan paets in the Evie hill when a golden plover flew over uttering its plaintive call. The old man looked up, listened to the call, then turned to his son saying 'Poor enough, God knows'.

Sweerie Stick

'Beuy are thoo ever pulled the sweerie stick?' The sweerie-stick was a stick used in an old game.*

The contestants sat on the floor facing each other with their feet against their partner's feet and pulled with both hands at a stick which was held transversely between them. This game was also played in Scotland where the same name was used for the stick.

Scots and Orkney dialect 'sweer' is lazy (allied to German 'schwer', difficult) and the idea behind the name of the game is that the stronger person pulls the 'lazy' person off the floor.

I sometimes play this game in gym with the pupils. It's a good game for upper primary pupils because with the greater physical development of girls at this stage it is usual for a girl to win, much to the chagrin of the boys!

Old games bring to mind the sport of 'flayan the cat'. It had nothing to do with maltreatment of cats. You grabbed a twartback, turned upside down and over and dropped to the ground. I can't explain the name of this game. I wonder if anyone can?

* a variation of this game was known in Sanday as the 'square tree'.

Spleuchan

On a bonny day I look across from Marwick to the hills of Sutherland. For over a thousand years the people at the other side of this stretch of water have spoken a different language and it should not surprise us greatly that words from Gaelic have infiltrated into our dialect.

Most of these have come through Scots — very common ones like 'sooans' and 'simmons'. Several people have sent me 'spleuchan' meaning purse from Gaelic 'spliùchan'.

I was intrigued by one definition which had its origin in Eday . . . 'a spleuchan is a skin purse made by Red Indians.' Many of these Red Indian spleuchans must have been brought to Orkney by men who worked for the Hudsons Bay Company. I wonder whether there are any of these old purses around still?

In Westray 'spleuchan' has the extended meaning 'an article of wood or wire hanging on the wall and having compartments for letters etc'. Probably such letter racks were originally made of leather.

Sook

During the last war letters were censored. An Orcadian couldn't even write about the weather: if he tried it the recipient of the letter would find a large chunk cut out of the page. Of course a letter from Orkney which made no mention of the weather made for pretty dull reading and many Orcadians could not tolerate such a handicap so when it came to describing weather conditions they resorted to dialect.

A woman wrote to her son in England saying, 'My hid's been makkan a right grand sook here the day' and immediately the son had a picture of a fine day with a comfortable breeze, dry brigstones and clotheslines flapping.

The origin of the word lies in Old Norse 'súgr', a draught of wind but really meaning a draught of drying wind. The Orcadian word retains the original meaning.

There was a family joke about an old man who got up very early, did some work outside, came in and announced to his family 'Weel bairns hid's makkan a bra sook on the hilltaps but hid's kinda slestry in the valleys'.

Suck

Last week we had 'sook' and this week 'suck' but of course I don't mean English 'suck' (which is pronounced 'sook'!).

'Suck' is a dialect word for straw or dry grass in a hen's nest in particular but also under an animal.*

A lady telephoned me to say that as a child she often had to go along the road verges in the spring of the year gathering suck for the hens' nests and a gentleman told me of a vanman who complained about the large number of broken eggs he had to handle: 'Hid's high time this weeman pat a gren more suck in the nests'.

Putting suck in the nests, like working with the hens generally was generally considered the role of the womenfolk.

The word 'suck' here is a puzzle. I think it's from the same root as last weeks word 'sook', a drying wind. It must mean 'grass etc. which has been dried by the wind'. We also speak of 'sookéd' fish, dried fish.

* many contributors rightly pointed out that there is another word 'suck' meaning mess, 'Whit a suck's aboot that ferm'. This 'suck' seems to be from a different root.

Fímro

This name is given to the velvet swimming crab in Shapinsay.

At one time considered a useless crab and thrown away, there is now a market for them outside Orkney. A fast moving crab which will give you a very sharp bite, it takes its name from the Old Norse word 'fimr,' quick.

Marwick recorded the name 'fimlar crab' in Evie for some unidentified type of crab; this could refer to the same animal. I wonder why the Old Norse names were not retained for shellfish?

'Humarr' meaning lobster is never recorded, the only relic of this word in our own dialect is 'homery', in poor condition with bones showing like a lobster.

'Partan' is a Gaelic word. The Gaels also call a partan 'rudhag' (literally 'red') and this possibly explains the Orkney word 'rudder' applied to a male crab.

A Westray man tells me that in Westray a 'fimro' is called an 'Englishman'. I wonder why.

Ootside-in

Orcadians speak a dialect of English filled with many odd phrases. 'Ootside-in' is one of them.

The English say 'inside-out' and the English form is more logical because we can see the inside when it's out but not the outside when it's in. 'Ootside-in' is one of the many reversed phrases found in our dialect.

Examples are 'headlight' for light headed, 'netting wire' for wire netting, 'needles and preens' for 'pins and needles'. There are countless other examples.

If you're a ferrylouper and you've noticed some unusual ones, let me know.

We also have many English words in our dialect which have different — even opposite meanings from English. If an Orcadian says he had had a 'frugal' meal he would have had plenty to eat: 'frugal' in English means sparing! A ferrylouping friend was a little put out to be told by her neighbour 'I wis annoyed when yi didna come ower last night as yi promised'. 'Annoyed' in Orkney dialect means 'concerned' or 'worried'!

Toomal

Many old farms have a field close by which they call the 'toomal'.

I have often been asked about this name: it means nothing to the modern farmer but they generally know it's one of the oldest fields on the farm.

The original Old Norse form was 'tún-völlr' and it specifically meant the homefield, not part of the run-rig system. It belonged to the adjacent dwelling as opposed to 'townsland' which was shared among farmers.

You might think it strange that the form 'tún-völlr' changes to 'toomal' but the explanation is straightforward. Firstly the final 'r' was never pronounced in this instance. Secondly a 'v' following an 'n' is difficult to pronounce so the 'n' gets changed to an 'm' and then the 'v' gradually drops out.

'Toomal' is found in a great variety of spellings in old deeds including the form 'tumult'!

Nirls

When I was very small one of my brothers came home and said he'd spoken to an old man who had told him 'they'd gotten the nirls in Harray'.

At a time when diptheria, scarlet fever and tuberculosis were rampant, the advent of 'nirls' sounded very ominous but mother explained it away as 'an owld word for chicken pox. The word was used in Scotland for skin eruptions generally.

In Shetland 'nirrels' was the word used for chicken pox and, according to Jakobsen it was also used for an illness which, according to his description, seems to be the mumps.

Another word for mumps in Orkney dialect was 'branks': the Scots also use branks in this sense but the real meaning of branks is a bridle or halter. Presumably the swollen neck suggested that branks were being worn.

In the 1920's when cat's whisker radios were in vogue, the user had to wear earphones. A Sandwick man was very annoyed when his neighbour whom he had visited sat all night with his earphones on. 'I couldna get a word oot o him', he said, 'he sat there aal night wi the muckle branks apin him'.

Madrom

'My his face wis just twitchan wi madrom'. 'Madrom' in Orkney means 'furious rage': in Shetland it means 'happiness' or 'hilarity'.

How does it come about that the same word is used for two completely different emotions?

To explain this we must think about the word 'mad' itself. In Orkney (and Scotland) the word is used in the sense 'angry'. In England it is used in the sense 'crazy' or in a milder form, 'stupid'. Linking the ideas rage, happiness and craziness is the idea of 'uncontrolled emotions'.

Although the word 'madrom' is known in Scotland its use is confined mainly to Orkney and Shetland. It seems to be a corrupted form of Scots 'wuidrim', madness from Old English 'wod', mad. Talking of 'madness' we must mention the common dialect word 'gyte', frequently used in the expression 'clean gyte' to describe someone who gets carried away with his emotions. The word is common in Scotland too.

Strangely enough no one has ever been able to explain its origin.

Teu-fa

This is a North Isles word for a 'lean-to' building. It falls into a group of Orkney words which we've discussed before in which words appear in reverse order. Remember 'ootside-in'?*

'Teu-fa' means 'to-fall' which in English means 'fall to' only English doesn't use that expression, English uses 'lean-to'. Scots however call such a building a 'fa-tae'!

We find a similar inversion in Scots 'pitten-tae' and Orkney dialect 'teu-pitten'. 'Whit can a buddy deu when a buddy's teu-pitten?' means 'what can one do in such trying circumstances?' But it's back to 'teu-fas' and related features.

'Biggan oan' is an Orcadian disease. There are few Orkney houses which don't have extensions, 'weengs' or porches. Even in olden days they had such things but they called them by different names. A 'gaviot' or 'givo' was a windbreak in front of a door, related to Norwegian 'gylve' a roofed passage. Another name for a gaviot was a 'bourtisement', a corruption of English 'bartisan'. The Old Norse name 'foreskin' (from 'forskygni') was also used for porch whereas forskal, yet another word for porch, came from the word 'forskáli'.

* see page 91

95

Sirpan

I was out with the pupils recently for a cycle run. Unfortunately, as so often happens in Orkney, a sudden and heavy shower drenched us.

A pupil came up to me and said, 'Me feet's just sirpan.' 'That's a right good Orkney word' I said, 'Whit wan?' he asked!

It's nearest relation is Norwegian 'sørpe', sludge or slush. In the south of Scotland the word 'sorp' to be soaked or drenched is used and I'm sure this is the same word. Another word used for 'soaking wet' in Orkney is 'sabbèd'.

'Whit a shooer o rain — I canna sit doon for me claes is just sabbèd'.

This word seems to be related to English 'sopping' wet. What a lot of 'watery noise' words begin with 's' in our dialect and indeed in English. How many of you have had a slerp of a kiss, have seen a slester, cleaned a sester or have been offended by a surgis of food in front of you?

Perhaps the 's' originally referred to the sound of moving water?

Whitemaa

This is such a common Orkney word. It is used for all birds of the gull family with the exception of the black-backed gull.

The 'white' element is obvious. The 'maa' element is from Old Norse 'már' a seagull but English also has the word 'mew' as in 'sea-mew'. The name comes from the call of the bird. It supposedly says 'maa' when it calls though Orcadians do not use this word for the call of the bird.

The call is 'cullya' and seagulls are often referred to as 'cullyas' in parts of Orkney. Orcadians believe that sheep say 'maa' whereas English believe they say 'baa'. The 'mew' of the cat is the same word as the 'mew' of the sea-mew. The 'mew' of the cat is also the same as the 'maa' of the sheep!

We can show this by reintroducing the word 'yarm' we referred to many weeks ago. North Ronaldsay people believe that sheep yarm, people on the Mainland believe that cats yarm.

As for the Old Norse they believed that sheep and birds yarmed! (Old Norse 'jarmr' to bleat or call).

Sluggermegullion

This, I think, is the longest word in Orkney dialect.

In the West Mainland of Orkney I picked up this word with the meaning 'a lazy person'. That same week I was down in South Ronaldsay and spoke to a lady who said 'I hiv a word that I baet yi don't ken the meaning o'. To my surprise, out came the word 'sluggermegullion' again pronounced in exactly the same way.

I offered the West Mainland definition but she wasn't too happy about that. She considered that the word applied rather to an untidy person. This word, like many others in our dialect is a hybrid.

The parent word was probably English 'slubber-degullion', a sloven but in Orkney the first element 'slubber' must have become confused with 'sluggard' and the 'de' corrupted to 'me'. Throughout English dialects there are many instances of long words being changed in this way.

Many Orcadians have for instance given me the word 'apstrapalous' for behaving in an angry and rough manner. The original English word is 'obstreperous' yet forms of this word with an 'l' in it are found throughout Britain.

Thee

Orkney and Shetland folk like their continental cousins use different words for 'you' according to whether the person being addressed is in their group of family and friends or outside it. 'Thoo' or 'thee' are used for familiar people and 'yi' for strangers or casual acquaintances.

At one time (and as late as the 1940's in Heddle and Harray) the pronunciation was 'doo' and 'dee' but these forms are found only in Shetland today.

Listen to the older Orcadian's perfect grammatical use of 'thoo' and 'thee'. 'Thoo' is used only for nominative singular, 'Thoo can go if thoo wants.' 'Thee' is used for vocative, accusative and dative cases. Here are examples of these cases: 'Ah'll tak thee wi me', 'Wait thee noo, hid's here somewey', 'Ah'm sure I gid thee hid'. Thee is also used as a possessive pronoun 'Tak thee things noo'.

After that diet of grammar, here is a little story from Harray at a time when the use of 'dee' and 'doo' forms were current. Two old ladies were arguing about the ownership of a pigeon (or 'doo') which intrigued a visitor. The elder of two ladies was affirmative it was her pigeon: 'Dat's no dee doo Dora, dee doo died'!

Jeck

A 'jeck' is a large tin mug. Sometimes they were referred to as 'mutchkin jecks'. To understand the origin of 'jeck' we have first of all to consider the English word 'jug'.

'Jug' was formerly used throughout Britain as a pet form of the girl's name 'Joan'. This girl's name in turn came to be applied also to a pitcher. Other drinking vessels were called 'Jacks' and 'Jills'.

Orkney dialect 'jeck' represents English 'Jack'. As for 'mutchkin' this is an old measure of capacity representing something less than half a litre.

The word mutchkin is used only in Scotland and must have come originally from Holland where the word 'mutse' was used for a measure of wine.

Index

aikaspire 16
amis 78
ando 55
anteran 14
arroo 74

blaggeran 49
bonnie words 10
bort 82
bratto 3
brett 76

clankan 29
cod 19
creepie 6
Cubbie Roo 70

dose 7
duffies 40

eerie-orms 63
eltit 67

fegs 18
fimro 90
frazzie 61

gablo 1
gamfer 32
girs 15
gittan 60
glessie 48
gurr 64
gutter 2

hallan 30
hen pen dirlo 45
hid 38
him-har 23
horse 44
horse-gok 69

imbian 79
ime 71

jeck 100

keero 58
kirsty-kringlo 56

lens metters 46
leufter 5
lippen 12
lokkars 62

madrom 94
meufy 9
miscone 52
morn (the) 35

neester 47
nilded 66
nirls 93

ossigar 8
ootside-in 91

plicko 17
plitterytildran 57
purwheer 42

queebeck 85

rittick 24
runnan raes 41

scootie 34
sirpan 96
skolder 51
skrek 11
skrue 73

skurt 13
skvandle 53
sluggermegullion 98
slygoose 65
sook 88
soolka 20
spleuchan 87
spret 33
spullyiereef 30
suck 89
surto 59
swee 39
sweenkle 83
sweerie stick 86

teebro 37
teeick 4
teu-fa 95
teultyir 43
thee 99
tishalago 54
toft 72
toomal 92
trimsan 76
trowy 75
tuction 29
tud 84
twartback 81

uivigar 28
unkan 26

vildroo 22

week(s) 80
whitema 97
whitna 36
wursum-mither 81

yamals 68
yarm 25
yeuk 50

Index